Processing Chicken

While Producing Winners

By Shaunta McDowell

Contents

Introduction 1

1 Letter to the CEO 6

2 Letter to a Production Supervisor 14

3 Begin with a Strategy to Win 18

4 The Fascinating Money Making Operation 21

5 The New Supervisor 26

6 Taking the Lead 34

7 The Motivated Employee 42

8 Being a Team Player 46

9 Superintendents Set the Tone 53

10 Points of Operation 58

11 Conflicts and Problem Solving 64

12 Four Point Management System for Retaining Hourly Employees 72

13 The Experienced Supervisor 75

Introduction

Some years ago, I went to one of my company's locations to assist new supervisors. I didn't like how the supervisors were being trained or how they were being treated. Our company was an excellent company to work for, but how could a new supervisor make it if they did not have adequate training, a support system, or the necessary information to get their jobs done? When I got back home from this location, I started to write about my journey as a supervisor. I wanted to write about the personal experiences that lead to me having a long-term career. My purpose in life is to help others and I wanted to use my experiences as a tool to do just that.

Having the knowledge of how you can win with your company is vital information. It gives you a reason to fight through adversity. Knowing your company's vision and having personal goals of your own pushes you to achieve those goals. The key to building a good team is to train everyone around you to follow the company rules and guidelines, and to do things right the first time. Being able to motivate and congratulate your team on their job performance will help you retain your employees.

I thought about why I came to my company and how I grew with my company—but most of all, I thought about the team that assisted me and excelled as a result. Even though we processed chicken, we produced winners! We all were flying high like eagles. I get excited just thinking about my journey!

Processing Chicken While Producing Winners is about the methods I have used to educate, motivate, and inspire others to win with their company. My journey was not easy, but it was necessary for me to understand how to help the next person. I had many people help me along the way within my company, including my husband, who went from an hourly employee to a manager. My division manager became the complex manager and my packing manager became the division manager. All of these individuals gave me a great start because they trained me and encouraged me. I was a part of their team and we were winners. I have had a great career.

I also wanted to use this book to encourage owners and CEOs to value every employee from the top to the bottom. People at this level can ensure high morale in the company through proper training and holding everyone to company standards. The morale within a company can make or break that organization. An owner or CEO has worked hard to grow their business. If they have someone running it who does not follow the ground rules or understand the company vision, it can set the company up for failure.

One day I walked into a restaurant and immediately noticed the restaurant had problems. It was eight o'clock in the morning and the front windows were dirty. As I walked in, no one was at the front station to greet me. This restaurant had a horrible smell even though the building was only a month old. I had been excited about eating there, but I was disappointed before I even got seated. I saw food and eating utensils on the floor. I started getting nervous about eating there. The menus the waitress brought us were dirty. I still ordered food because I believed in this company.

The last straw was when my food came to the table and it had hair in it. I asked for the manager and the manager sent the assistant in training out to help me. But I wanted the manager. I didn't want to talk about the food—I wanted the manager to know everything I saw from the moment I walked in the door. The manager came out and was very rude. He didn't care that I was a costumer and that the owner was losing money because of his lack of leadership skills.

I left the restaurant and wrote an email to the company immediately. The email was titled YOU ARE ONE STEP CLOSER TO CLOSING YOUR DOORS. This was a Sunday morning and the owner of the business responded to the email immediately. I couldn't believe it. I was not expecting a response but I got one. This person owned not only a chain of these restaurants but also a huge corporation that consisted of other restaurants, hotels, and hospitals. He had come to America with a few dollars in his pocket and worked his way through school and had become a multimillionaire.

He asked me what he could do to improve his business and I gave him my ideas freely because I wanted this business to make it. The area needed those jobs as much as he wanted to keep his business open. The owner got me in touch with his regional manager and the company president. I wasn't surprised that the flaws of that location started with those two men. They were nowhere near the site when I came to the restaurant but the training they gave left a lasting impression. All they talked about was who was getting fired; neither of them mentioned who would be getting trained. These two men had been with this company only briefly, and it was obvious. They had absolutely nothing invested. The regional manager asked me how my email skipped all the proper chains to go straight to the owner. I told him I guessed the owner was the only person who cared enough to respond to it.

I tell this story because owners and CEOs who have invested time, money, and sweat into their business should be concerned. They should want passionate employees working for their company who care about all aspects of the business. Owners and CEOs have the power to change things. Vision, dedication, hard work, and teamwork are all necessary to grow a company—but good training is essential. Proper training is the key to avoiding unnecessary losses.

Chapter 1: Letter to the CEO

Dear CEO,

I felt that it was necessary to write you this letter because of the great things I have heard about you personally and because of your work ethic. I was told you come to work early and you actually check all of your own emails. Being confident in what I know, and knowing you care about this company and the employees who are a part of your team, motivated me to reach out to you.

First of all, this letter will not be short because you don't know me. During my time as a production supervisor, I went to a sister location to train a new supervisor. I noticed how hurt and frustrated many of the supervisors seemed, due to numerous reasons but mainly due to bad management. I could see the same hurt spreading to the employees, which meant it was expanding to their communities, churches, businesses, and going home to their family members.

Those supervisors didn't know what I knew. They didn't know that our company was a gold mine of opportunity for both the most educated person and the person with no education at all. And they would never know, because all of them had already given up and would eventually quit.

I came to my company as an eighteen-year-old woman. I almost had to be dragged here. I didn't want to work at a chicken processing plant. At that age, I couldn't see past the chicken. I couldn't see that the chicken was money that looked like chicken.

In everything you do, you start with a *why*. My *why* was that I had a two-year-old child to provide for and I wanted a better life for her. Just four years before I started to work for my company, I was in the foster care system. I knew that when I graduated high school I would have to join the military or find a job to take care of my child and my family. The military was out because I could not even think about leaving my child.

My part-time job was income, but I needed a job with benefits—and my company had them. As the company prospered, so did I. After working for the company a year, I realized I wanted to own something and my supervisor told me about a way I could buy a home. I was educated by my supervisors daily and I listened most of the time. Because I listened to them, at nineteen years old, I signed the papers for my mortgage.

I took my mother with me to the signing and she was scared because no one in our family had ever owned anything. She asked me how I was going to pay the loan back. I told her I didn't know how, but I was going to pay it. Her fear began to discourage me—but I wanted my child to have a place she could call home. I told my mom to wait for me in the lobby and I finished the loan process.

I told you that story to let you know that if I would have listened to my mother discouraging me because of her fear, I may not have become the person I am today. But my supervisor told me I could own something, and I believed it. This event changed my *why*. Now my *why* was because I was a homeowner and I had to provide for my daughter.

After I bought the house, I started to look at what I did differently. I wanted to do the best job I could. I wanted to be successful within my company because my company was growing. A couple of years later, a superintendent and a manager saw something in me that I didn't see in myself and they gave me the opportunity to become a supervisor. My manager changed my entire frame of mind and my life.

I have invested twenty years of my life into this business and I am confident in what I know. I have never been afraid to give my opinion, to make a decision, or to be held accountable. I was trained to push through challenges and to learn from my mistakes. Every year we watched a recording of a motivational speaker who would teach and train us how to treat employees. I don't recall the speaker mentioning that they were ever a supervisor.

Most of our company's vision statement clearly states who we are and how we should act. As managers and supervisors, we should be a dedicated team of caring individuals. *Dedicated* meaning we come to work and do the jobs we are required to do, and do our very best. *Caring* meaning we care about our jobs, we care about our employees, and we care about the product we send out.

You will never get individuals to be dedicated if they don't care. You have to train employees, give them what they need, and give them a clear understanding of what is expected of them. Supervisors need the same thing.

I am positive, sir, that your company has given you the resources you need to get your job done. It goes back to caring and being dedicated. In our plant, it took only one person in a higher position not doing their job to lose money for the other 1400 people that worked there. The person in the higher position was directing the show. That's why proper training is necessary so that knowledge can be passed down from manager, to middle manager, to supervisor, to hourly employee.

My eyes and my hands serve two different purposes for my body, but I need them all and they are equally important to me. That is how every manager, superintendent, supervisor, and hourly employee should feel. All companies must give middle management the very best training in the beginning because they come into contact with a lot of people but are only responsible for managing a few. Middle managers are the people between the supervisors and upper management. They communicate the information from upper management to supervisors. Middle managers often volunteer in their communities as coaches and youth leaders and can brand their company's name either good or bad.

It is absolutely necessary for middle managers to be knowledgeable as well as good communicators. Middle managers train the supervisors and the supervisors train the employees. Trained employees turn into passionate employees because they have mastered something. I was trained well by my manager and it resulted in me being successful on the job and also in other areas. I am so passionate about my company that when I have a problem, my thought process compels me to find the root of the problem and fix it. This is how everyone should feel. I have learned to tackle problems with ideas and suggestions.

I have never seen finger pointing fix a problem, but I have seen finger pointing create problems. I was taught to find the problem, involve the most knowledgeable people to help fix the problem, and train others in order to limit the chance of the problem happening again.

Most companies have all the talent and experience that they need to accomplish tasks. They also have the talent and experience to excel higher than their competitors. Most companies have a solid foundation in their company's vision statement, mission statement, and ground rules. I am almost certain that when the owners were thinking of this company, their mission was not just to make money but also to motivate the success of others. Because successful employees end up being long-term employees.

Today if you asked me my *why*, I would tell you I care about what I do, I believe in my company, and my company has given me and the employees in my area an opportunity to become homeowners, business owners, and stock owners. My company has trained me with skills to advance and be successful in other areas. My company has taken me from teen mom to college grad's mom. My company has given me the opportunity to work for twenty years. This is what inspired me to write *Processing Chicken While Producing Winners*. I want everyone to be as proud as I am to work for a Fortune 500 company and to educate management on plant/employee relationships. I am proof that you can start from anywhere, and with good leadership you can excel with any company.

No company should want to lose experienced employees because of bad management. My goal is to make a difference in your company by making sure that middle managers are trained. Don't lose valuable experience because of poor middle management. Poor middle management can cause division, confusion, and frustration. In the next fourteen chapters I will take the opportunity to train middle managers and supervisors. This training will make a major difference in your company's bottom line by giving management a good understanding of how to retain employees and train good supervisors.

Questions for CEOs to Consider

1. Are you concerned with your bottom line?

2. Do you want your company to become the number one company?

3. Are you giving your management team everything they need to be successful?

4. Does everyone in your company feel like a winner?

5. Do you want to retain your employees?

Chapter 2: Letter to a Production Supervisor

If I could have read this book when I started in management, I would have been more patient. I would have looked at the big picture—financial security—but realized that financial security comes at a price. During my first few years at the company, I had to learn a lot of different jobs. I had no idea that the variety of jobs I was doing would later set me up for success at my organization. The countless hours, days away from my family, and moments of uncertainty framed my world. I could understand things that most people I worked with every day could not understand, because I paid the price to gain that experience by learning those jobs and skills and working in different parts of the company.

In the twenty years I have worked for my company, the world has changed. Although things are very different, one thing will remain the same: production supervisors are responsible for the employees they supervise. We are necessary for our employees and our company to survive any market change. Supervisors train, motivate, coach, and hold employees accountable.

As a supervisor, you may have to deal with managers who are educated on *what* needs to be done, but who lack the actual knowledge of *how* to get the job done. Management can easily calculate what a supervisor needs to do but forget to factor in different aspects such as how all the employees may be new and it may take them longer to get the job done, or what happens when several employees are absent at once. These are variances a supervisor will have to factor in when setting goals.

Your direct manager might be terrible sometimes, but that does not mean you should be. You should follow your company guidelines, because you work for the company. Employees live up to the environment their supervisor creates. Supervisors, if you break the rules and show a lack of concern on the job, this is the environment you are creating for your employees. If you follow the rules, show you have concern for your employees, and are fair, you will create a positive working environment for your employees. Create an environment where *you* would like to come to work every day instead of one where you are so frustrated that you frustrate everyone around you.

When employees get frustrated, they quit. As a supervisor, you should set a goal to *train* employees and *retain* employees. This will involve you learning what your employees are capable of and knowing how to encourage them when things change. Supervisors have to know their people. They have to be fair but firm and hold employees accountable only after they have been trained.

In my many years of being a production supervisor I have trained hundreds of people. I even receive phone calls from coworkers in different states. I have been asked so many questions that I felt compelled to write this book.

I am by no means trying to impose my views on anyone. My perceptions are a direct result of my own life experiences. I am sharing my experiences with you in the hope that you will have a successful career as a production supervisor. I am 100 percent sure your company has given you all the tools and resources you need to become successful. Use them effectively and success is certain. I have gone from teen mom to homeowner, stock owner, business consultant, business owner, and author.

Points for Production Supervisors to Ponder

1. Know your *why* and have a win/win attitude.

2. Know your company's benefits.

3. Know your company's vision, mission, and ground rules.

4. Write a list of your long-term and short-term goals.

5. Put the time in and don't take any time for granted.

Chapter 3: Begin with a Strategy to Win

First of all, in anything you do, you have to begin with a strategy to win. In order to believe in your personal mission you have to know *why* you have chosen your career path. Know your *why*. My *why* was because I had a child and I was a single mother. My company had good wages and benefits for the area, and I needed the income.

Most people who have come to work for my company are just like I was—they only thought about the pay. People in higher positions might disagree with this fact, but I have known countless individuals who did not know what benefits the company had to offer. If it were not for my supervisors teaching me, I would not have understood my benefits.

Everything most companies have to offer is a reward to you for your hard work. Benefits should motivate you to do well, but you can't get motivated if you don't know what your company has to offer. I had several instances where individuals were shocked to learn that our company had been in operation for many years and hundreds of employees had worked there. They thought the company started with them. After we discussed the positives of the company and the benefits offered, I explained the company culture. This

Points for Production Supervisors to Ponder

1. Know your *why* and have a win/win attitude.

2. Know your company's benefits.

3. Know your company's vision, mission, and ground rules.

4. Write a list of your long-term and short-term goals.

5. Put the time in and don't take any time for granted.

Chapter 3: Begin with a Strategy to Win

First of all, in anything you do, you have to begin with a strategy to win. In order to believe in your personal mission you have to know *why* you have chosen your career path. Know your *why*. My *why* was because I had a child and I was a single mother. My company had good wages and benefits for the area, and I needed the income.

Most people who have come to work for my company are just like I was—they only thought about the pay. People in higher positions might disagree with this fact, but I have known countless individuals who did not know what benefits the company had to offer. If it were not for my supervisors teaching me, I would not have understood my benefits.

Everything most companies have to offer is a reward to you for your hard work. Benefits should motivate you to do well, but you can't get motivated if you don't know what your company has to offer. I had several instances where individuals were shocked to learn that our company had been in operation for many years and hundreds of employees had worked there. They thought the company started with them. After we discussed the positives of the company and the benefits offered, I explained the company culture. This

Points for Production Supervisors to Ponder

1. Know your *why* and have a win/win attitude.

2. Know your company's benefits.

3. Know your company's vision, mission, and ground rules.

4. Write a list of your long-term and short-term goals.

5. Put the time in and don't take any time for granted.

Chapter 3: Begin with a Strategy to Win

First of all, in anything you do, you have to begin with a strategy to win. In order to believe in your personal mission you have to know *why* you have chosen your career path. Know your *why*. My *why* was because I had a child and I was a single mother. My company had good wages and benefits for the area, and I needed the income.

Most people who have come to work for my company are just like I was—they only thought about the pay. People in higher positions might disagree with this fact, but I have known countless individuals who did not know what benefits the company had to offer. If it were not for my supervisors teaching me, I would not have understood my benefits.

Everything most companies have to offer is a reward to you for your hard work. Benefits should motivate you to do well, but you can't get motivated if you don't know what your company has to offer. I had several instances where individuals were shocked to learn that our company had been in operation for many years and hundreds of employees had worked there. They thought the company started with them. After we discussed the positives of the company and the benefits offered, I explained the company culture. This

gave them a different perspective. They felt motivated to take their position in the company and felt proud to be a part of a successful organization.

Once I knew how I could be rewarded, I started to study the company vision. Often people will do a job every day for years without knowing the vision of their company. If you know your company's vision, you will know what the company is trying to accomplish. If you begin with wanting to be successful with this vision you will work harder to accomplish it.

The very day you agree to work for your company, you *become* the company. This is especially true if the company has an employee stock ownership program. You should want to put out a good wholesome product because you are a stock owner. You should want to increase the value of the shareholders' stock. Who is the shareholder? You are! This will also benefit your employees because once you know, then you can always use this to motivate them later.

Who would have thought that twenty years later I would still be with the same company? I have to thank God for sending me a production manager and a division manager who saw potential in me. These two men taught me how to help myself as a supervisor. They also taught me how to be responsible for my actions and how to hold others accountable for their actions. If I could go back, I would capitalize on every opportunity I had.

Chapter 3 Questions to Consider

1. Do you know why you are working for your company?

2. Do you feel motivated to perform well?

3. Do you know your company's vision statement?

4. Is your company's vision achievable?

5. Are you a shareholder?

Chapter 3 Points to Ponder

1. Know your *why*.

2. Know your company's benefits.

3. Know your company's culture.

4. Know your company's vision.

5. Become your company.

Chapter 4: The Fascinating Money Making Operation

I remember the day I walked into the plant twenty years ago. I was an eighteen-year-old single parent who had finished high school only five months earlier. I had worked at a fast food restaurant my entire senior year. The poultry plant paid more and also had the potential for pay raises.

The plant was so big, and it looked very strange to me to see raw whole chickens hanging on a line. At that moment, I could not see a future for myself in this facility. I wanted to run as fast I could to get out of there. Those same chickens would later be converted to dollar bills in my life—a stable future with benefits and growth.

Then, I had no idea this was an industry I could profit from; therefore, I went to work and just worked. I never studied my company's vision, I didn't know what my benefits were, and I didn't see the process as being a fascinating, money-making operation. This lack of knowledge probably caused me thousands of dollars. I didn't walk through the door with a win/win attitude; I came knowing I needed to work but not knowing how to let the work benefit me.

I started in a department that everyone told horror stories about, but my experience was one of personal growth. My supervisor had started out on the line just like me. The first thing my supervisor recognized was that his employees had to be trained how to do things the correct way. If you are a person who is responsible for other employees, help yourself by making sure they get trained the correct way. There is no way I would have made it if I hadn't been trained by a knowledgeable supervisor at the beginning.

My supervisor also knew that once he trained employees, he had to hold them accountable. He made sure his employees knew they were accountable. My supervisor did not cut corners. I worked on the line for five years before I would get the chance to move up and move on. The thing that made me want to try harder was that, while my company was growing and becoming more successful, so was I. At age nineteen, I purchased my first home. I did this after having worked at my company for only one year. At this point I wanted and needed more. I started to look around at how things worked and I thought about ways I could make the job easier.

The very first thing I realized was that all employees were linked whether we liked it or not. From the person selling the product to the person processing the product, we were linked. I decided right then that I was going to become my company. I had no idea that making this decision would help me prosper. I decided I was going to think outside the box.

I worked next to some people who didn't care one bit about doing their job. I was not one of those employees. I didn't fit in and I wanted my company to grow because my company was me. I felt a sense of ownership.

If you are a supervisor, don't ever think you don't have hourly employees who will try to get out of work. I have seen employees work while the supervisor was there and stop working the minute the supervisor turned their back. This upset me; therefore, I did everything I could to keep the line going whether the supervisor was there or not. This got the attention of one of my supervisors, who promoted me to a lead position.

My main job as a lead was to keep the line running smoothly. In a poultry plant, you need to have clean, organized areas. If your lead person does not understand the process, they will not understand how to help keep things in order. This is a mistake I have seen in more areas than mine. Information is the key. You can be a supervisor but you can also educate your employees on the process. While educating your employees, they will help you catch mistakes. My co-workers hated me as a lead person at first until I showed them an easier way to do the job. We would pack product and conduct races while doing it. The day would go by so fast and the work would still get done. We really didn't have an easier job, we just worked together and made it easier. Mindset and motivation made the difference.

My job performance as a lead person got the attention of a superintendent. He saw the fire in me and believed in me more than I believed in myself. I was offered a supervisor position a couple of times before I accepted it. I thought I was too young to take on that kind of responsibility. I was twenty-three years old when I decided the time was right to take a supervisor job.

Oh my God! I was in for a rude awakening.

Chapter 4 Questions to Consider

1. Are you expecting a stable future with your company?

2. Do you know your company's benefits and do you understand how they can work for you?

3. Do you think you have had proper training?

4. Do you expect to be held accountable after you are trained?

5. Do you educate your employees?

Chapter 4 Points to Ponder

1. Study your company's vision.

2. Start learning the minute you walk in the door.

3. Stay positive. Don't let negative people discourage you with negative opinions.

4. Take advantage of every opportunity you have.

5. Information is the key.

Chapter 5: The New Supervisor

I knew how to be a lead person, but supervision was another ball game. I thought I understood everything but it turns out I didn't have a clue. As a supervisor, I was responsible for safety, production, cost, efficiency, and so many other things.

The area I was put in to supervise was new to me. I had some knowledge of what the department did but for the most part I was new to the operation. The very first person I was placed with to train me was the supervisor in that department. I would be his co-worker for the next eight months.

Have you ever been around a person who wanted to have control over everything but didn't want to take responsibility for anything? I will just say that working with this guy was difficult. I had coworkers who were a nuisance when I was an hourly employee, but when you give a person some authority and they think that they know everything, it can be difficult.

The first few months I worked with this man, I basically worked as his lead person. The advantage I had was that I was learning as much as I could learn. If you are a supervisor, do not ever miss a chance to learn. At this time I knew nothing about technical supervision, but my packing manager and division manager gave me tips almost daily. I wanted to give up every day because I didn't understand how the process in my department ran—and I had a coworker that didn't know how to train me.

From this experience, there were several things I learned *not* to do. The first thing I noticed was that my coworker showed favoritism. Even when I was an hourly employee, I knew this was not right. I saw him treat employees in higher paid positions differently. This guy was not a team player but I needed him. He knew more than I did, and the hourly employees went to him for everything. I put all my time and energy into learning what he knew and learning what everybody in our department should be doing.

The more I worked with this guy the more that I despised the way he did things. The department was in total chaos all the time. I used to think to myself *Why in the world would anyone want to do this job—even if the pay was good and the benefits were great?*

My lack of experience drained me mentally, but I was like a sponge. I kept learning. I asked questions about anything that would affect the team. I would come to work two hours early and stay two hours after the shift was over. I was determined to learn everything about our department. Trust me, if you don't know what you are doing, putting in the time to learn will benefit you later.

After about eight months of playing assistant coach to my coworker, a mishap occurred in the department. I was given written notice that I was directly responsible for this mishap and was informed of the consequences if this incident should occur again. A light bulb went off in my head: I was not being treated like an assistant in this written notice, so why was I working like an assistant? I decided from that day forward I would develop a take-charge attitude. I figured *how in the world could I get disciplined again without trying to make things better?* My personal mission from that day forward was to do the best job I could do for the company.

The very next day I started to change the way we did things. I was already trained on how to discipline employees—in the past eight months I had been the disciplinarian for about a hundred people. Next, I had to get a process set up that would help our department run efficiently. Neither my coworker nor the employees wanted to change anything they were doing. They didn't care that the department was a mess, that some of them worked overtime every day, and that the cost was high. They were so accustomed to seeing things being run badly, they eventually thought what they saw every day was the correct way to do things.

Changing the way my team did things was hard. Once employees get used to something, they expect it to stay the same way. But anyone who knows anything about business will tell you that you have to constantly try new things to keep up with competitors—especially if what you are doing is not working for the company.

The first change I made was a small one, but it showed my coworker that I had arrived as a supervisor. Instead of us working together to see if my idea would work, he immediately attempted to change it back. He was okay with me disciplining employees and also okay with me taking responsibility for his actions—but he had a problem with me using my brain to make decisions on how our team should operate. I went right in and changed it back to my way again. And I knew it was time to communicate with my coworker so that we could solve some of our team's problems.

That's when everything I had been holding in for the last eight months came out. I explained to him that if I was going to be responsible for anything, I was going to use my authority as supervisor to find a more effective and efficient way to get our job done.

He didn't understand what I had in me. I had been a lead person and an hourly employee and I had trained all of our department employees for the last eight months. I knew what wasn't working now and that it was time for a change. He wasn't having it. He did not want anything to change. I told him if he didn't want to use my idea, he was going to have to go get someone with more authority than we had to make me change it back.

So that is exactly what he did. I didn't care. I wanted our manager to know there was a huge problem that was costing our company money. I was armed with the research I had done and the trials I had run without my coworker knowing. He underestimated how smart I was from the beginning when I couldn't understand why he didn't want to work as a team. He didn't care about improving our jobs and our company—which goes back to that dedication we discussed earlier. No one could give him that; it has to come from within. He never asked me my opinion, he never asked me about my background, he only told me what to do and assisted me in getting it done.

When our manager came, he let my coworker know that my change was fine and told him we were going to try it. Unlike my coworker, our manager didn't mind change. He had an open mind. This infuriated my coworker. This was the first of many disagreements we had until I finally asked our manager if he could separate the department. This would mean that we would split the responsibility of supervising the team. He would have fifty employees and I would have fifty. My coworker went crazy, telling our manager he did not want to split the responsibilities and he did not want to separate the team. Of course he didn't. He didn't want to be held accountable for anything.

My coworker was nowhere near the type of supervisor I wanted to become. I wanted to be a great supervisor that could tackle responsibility head on, not run from it. My manager told me he would grant my wish and separate the team. My coworker quit the same day—and it would be a long time before I got another coworker. I was now responsible for supervising one hundred employees on my own and it was definitely a challenge. It was time to get a plan—and in order to succeed, I needed to call on everything I had in me.

As a supervisor, you have to understand your responsibilities. Sometimes you will come across a person in a higher position who doesn't have a clue how to train you. You need to stay calm and evaluate the situation.

The very first thing you have to learn is your points of operation. Points of operation are any points that affect your departmental goals. When you learn your points of operation, you will learn how to fix problems or eliminate them. In the department I supervised, I had four points of operation: the front of the machine, the back of the machine, someone to pull the product to get credit for my product, and the person to calculate it. The other people in the department were my points of operation support. I utilized my support to keep my points of operation going.

Support can come in all forms—employees, supervisors, superintendents, managers, owners, and outside resources. You should never think you are on your own. You will never know what information someone can give you if you don't ask.

Learn as much as you can about your job and the positions that affect your job. This will help you have a good understanding of what you need to be successful. If you are not successful, your company will lose big.

Chapter 5 Questions to Consider

1. Do you know and understand your responsibilities?

2. Are you learning as much as you can with every opportunity you have?

3. Can you answer basic questions directly related to your department?

4. Are you putting in extra effort to learn?

5. Are you utilizing all the skills and knowledge you have within yourself and do you know how to utilize them?

6. Do you want to have a successful career and advance in your personal life?

Chapter 5 Points to Ponder

1. Learn as much as you can.

2. Never show favoritism.

3. Know your position.

4. Learn everything about your department .

5. Do your research and run trials.

Chapter 6: Taking the Lead

Clearly, things changed for my employees after my coworker quit. I was younger than any employee in my department and the employees had just lost the only supervisor they felt comfortable talking to. I didn't understand this at the time, but your employees have to know that they can trust you, that you are dependable, and that you care about them as people, not just workers.

My communication skills were terrible and the department was still in chaos. Each day I came to work, I had a new battle. The battles were tough because it seemed to my employees that I was changing everything they were accustomed to doing.

Some of those employees had been doing their job for a number of years. I didn't know at the time that I had to motivate my employees as I trained them to do things correctly. They all had gotten used to things being done differently from how they should have been done, and my efforts to train them caused anger and frustration. My group had been trained wrong and needed to be retrained according to the company policies. I trained them, trained them, and trained them. I quickly noticed that a lot of them had never been supervised. This was a huge problem.

Even though I had been in the department with them for a number of months, I spent the majority of that time learning their jobs. I had only recently learned how to actually supervise them. A supervisor has to train employees, motivate them, and hold them accountable. You can't hold someone accountable when they weren't trained correctly. Supervisors should monitor and correct employees when they do not meet job requirements.

I started to pay really close attention to what everyone was doing. I knew by now what they should be doing but had to make sure they were really doing their assigned jobs correctly. I quickly found out the areas that were going to give me problems. Those areas were making my job difficult by the minute. Every day I would go home very tired and mentally frustrated because I could not figure things out.

I decided to take the entire operation and run it as if everyone was in the same position. If you know anything about football, you know that everyone can't be a quarterback or a running back. The same thing went for my team. Everyone couldn't play in the same position. A supervisor should be able to recognize skills in their employees. This means that you have to take the time to get to know your employees.

During this time there was one hourly employee who came to me and showed me the things that I didn't know about the department. She showed me things I couldn't see because of my position as a supervisor. This employee had been with the company for a number of years and she had worked in numerous positions. She was passionate about her job and she cared about her job as much as I cared about mine.

My other employees did not have a relationship with me but they knew this lady and they respected her. I hadn't earned their respect; therefore, I was getting none. The fact that I was their supervisor didn't mean anything. My employees treated me as if I didn't know enough to tell them what to do.

As this employee showed me things, I couldn't understand why she worked in her current position instead of applying for a higher position. She was the department scale operator but she had so much potential. I decided that I would train her to be a lead person.

On my team, the lead person was the arms and legs of the operation. Everyone on the team was stationary except the lead people. I trained my lead people to do every job in the department so that they could relieve employees. I also trained my lead people the process in which the team was run. I needed lead people who could completely understand the function of the entire team. They were the only employees who could move and they needed to know where to go without my telling them. Lead people also had to be dependable and follow the work rules. In the course of delegating jobs and holding people accountable, I started to recognize potential in them. I started to build my team.

Some employees had knowledge of things that would benefit the company in many ways. I prepared almost every lead person I had to be a supervisor. I taught them things without giving them too much authority. My lead person had a sneak peek into what I did as a supervisor because she usually talked to me more than any other employee did.

As I said before, I have always thought of everyone who worked for the company being a part of a linked chain. If the chain was broken, no one would be successful. I noticed some people in my industry didn't see things this way and failure was written all over their operation.

My method was if a person was trained to do a job and could do the job, they become an individual who has mastered something. Therefore they specialized in what they have mastered. Now let me make this clear to all you supervisors: **Just because an employee may physically show another employee how to do a job does not release you from training your employee**. Supervisors have to make job requirements clear and monitor employee progress.

Supervisors who don't like to spend time in their departments will cause confusion for their employees because their employees need them. The better the supervisor trains the employee, the better chance the employee will stay.

I had employees come in and go right back out when I first became a supervisor. I would have given up, too, if I hadn't been trained—I was so confused about what I had to do. But I started to let my specialized employees assist me in training new hires. This worked for me, and my turnover rate started to decrease. Some of the specialized employees even started to take on more responsibility and excelled in getting the daily job done.

I began to talk to my employees and ask them about their long term goals. I began to let some of them know that they could be in the same position as I was. Our company was always looking for people to grow our company who were motivated, determined, hardworking individuals who could manage others.

During this time I encouraged my scale operator, who had become a lead person, to apply for an open salaried position. She looked at me and said "I don't know if I can do it." I told her she could. She then said she didn't want to leave me. I told her she had to leave where she was because the company needed her experience. Then I reminded her of how we would start up together, organize the team together, and end the day together. I came to her team with little knowledge of what was going on but she taught me the things she knew—even though I was her supervisor.

She learned with an open mind and she worked hard. I never saw her as someone who was leaving me. I saw her as someone who was on my team, who was given a chance to be promoted, and who was knowledgeable enough to excel at the job.

You are only as successful as the people around you. My attitude was that everyone should be winning. Some employees loved their positions and wanted to stay in them, but they were still winning because they loved what they did. Those employees had job security; therefore, they were excelling in their personal lives. They were purchasing homes, providing for their families, and planning for retirement.

My team saw things happen that we never knew were possible. Things got better because everyone knew they were a part of the team. Every employee in every position felt important.

Chapter 6 Questions to Consider

1. Do you communicate well with your employees, superintendents, and managers?

2. Do you know how to train your employees?

3. Do you know the job duties of everyone in your department, and have you explained them to your employees?

4. Do you have all of your employees in the right position and do you know how to recognize ability and skill?

5. Do you let your employees know they all are important to the company's success?

6. Have you explained to your employees how working for the company can benefit them?

Chapter 6 Points to Ponder

1. Learn about your employees by having conversations with them.
2. Recognize individual talent and abilities.

3. Train your employees correctly, give them what they need to do the job, and be consistent. If you are not consistent, your employees won't be either.

4. Disciplinary action should always be an instructional tool. An employee should be talked to first about an incident. You should never be upset when using the company policies. The employee should have a clear understanding of what is expected of them and know what the next action will be.

5. Congratulate, motivate, and inspire your employees. Give them a win/win attitude, make them feel a part of the team, and encourage them just as much as you supervise them.

Chapter 7: The Motivated Employee

As I recognized potential in my employees, I started to listen to their opinions. Sometimes as supervisors we think we know everything and that just because we do something a certain way, it has been done that way forever. Actually, if a person specializes in a job, they have usually mastered everything about it including taking care of the problems. I have always known that trying something different can be good or bad. Sometimes change can scare you—but if you don't try, you won't know if it will benefit you or your department.

I never thought for a minute that everything that I did was right, but I was stubborn. I had an hourly employee who asked me every day if he could train to be a lead person. I was unsure about letting him try, because the position he was in didn't have as much responsibility. He was young and motivated but I wasn't sure if I should take a chance on him. He was not asking for more pay; just for more responsibility because he wanted to train to be a lead person. This young man came to work on time every day. He had even started training to do other things I had no idea that he knew how to do.

On my team, the lead person had to be dependable and responsible and have good communication skills. I decided to give this employee a chance and wanted to make sure that he received the best possible training. He was motivated and I wanted to set him up to be successful. I put him with someone who specialized in being a lead person. His trainer was older and the best individual to train him. The trainer did things the way that they should be done. He was dependable, hardworking, and had great communication skills. He was also eager to train this young man because he had a good working relationship with him. If you were going to be a lead person, this trainer was the person to give you the tools that you needed to succeed.

I was amazed to see what happened with this motivated employee when I gave him more responsibility. This young man was dependable, consistent, and hard working. Sometimes he was hard headed, but only because he wanted to be the best. I was thankful to have an employee who was eager to learn and happy with what he was doing.

The young man went on to become a supervisor. I was happy for him because he cared about what he did and had a passion for it. I thought of this as growth for me. I was surrounding myself with people who had mastered their jobs and others who had the will to learn more and take on more responsibility. We were all on a path to success. I had dependable people around me that I could trust. We were winning.

Chapter 7 Questions to Consider

1. Are you afraid to change your employee's work positions?

2. Do you feel like you have employees who specialize at their job?

3. Do you have any motivated employees?

4. Do you know how to train a motivated employee to become successful?

5. Are you surrounding yourself with a team of employees with winning attitudes?

Chapter 7 Points to Ponder

1. Listen to your employees—because you don't know everything.

2. Never be afraid to give motivated employees more responsibility.

3. Give motivated employees more responsibility only after they have mastered their assigned job. These employees should be dependable, responsible, and show good character.

4. Encourage motivated employees and pair them with other employees who they can relate to for training.

5. Never hinder an employee's career growth. Challenge the motivated employee while giving them an understanding of their job duties. Encourage them when they make mistakes and guide them in the right direction.

Chapter 8: Being a Team Player

To be a part of any winning team you have to have patience, you have to communicate, you have to compromise, you have to respect each other, and you have to be loyal. This almost sounds like a marriage—but I see my coworkers more than I see my family at times. After working with a group of people for twenty years it was just like a marriage.

Effective team players know they have to communicate information to the entire team on what has to be done. Each supervisor involved with an assignment needs to have a clear understanding of what they need to get done. I have seen teams take responsibility for getting an assignment done without the supervisor having any knowledge of it. That means the middle manager did not communicate with the supervisor.

First of all, it is rude not to tell the direct supervisor. Second, the supervisor is responsible for their employees—how can they hold their employees accountable if they don't know what they should be doing? I see this too many times in production. The communication is bad and it causes more problems and confusion than I care to deal with.

How could these supervisors train their employees when they did not have the proper training? These supervisors were tired and frustrated. Our company did not operate this way; we believed in giving all of our employees the tools that they needed to get the job done. Our company wanted their employees to be successful and this individual was doing things his way and in the process he was affecting lives. He was young and inexperienced. He needed training. He was superior to me but I still felt like I had to tell him that he was not following the company vision statement. But this man was stubborn. He did not have respect for his coworkers, nor was he loyal to our company. He did things the way he wanted to, with little care for or patience with his new supervisors.

I stopped talking to him and went into my designated area and worked with the supervisor there. I spoke with each and every one of his hourly employees on the first day I was there. I found out so much about them, and their supervisor did, too. These employees had skills that were very useful. One of them was from a city near my home and his supervisor never knew. I was twelve hours away from my home and I was standing in front of an employee who was from an area less than an hour from my home. His supervisor never knew because he had never had a conversation with this employee.

Later, the supervisor and I ate lunch with his coworkers. I had never seen a group of people who looked so sad. They were sad because every day they came to work they felt like failures, never winning. The morale was so low. It wasn't because of our company; it was because of their untrained superintendent. He didn't understand that what he was doing was giving our company a bad name.

Before I left this location, I gave some of the supervisors my number and encouraged them to call me whenever they had a question or needed encouragement. I knew it would be hard for them to continue working for our company. They were not getting the training and support they needed, so they didn't feel they were a part of our team.

Teammates train together, strategize together, play together, lose together, and win together. The coach leads the team. How can you win the game with a coach who does not follow the rules of the game? How can you win with a coach that does not want to play with the team? You can't win because you don't have what it takes to win.

5. Never hinder an employee's career growth. Challenge the motivated employee while giving them an understanding of their job duties. Encourage them when they make mistakes and guide them in the right direction.

Chapter 8: Being a Team Player

To be a part of any winning team you have to have patience, you have to communicate, you have to compromise, you have to respect each other, and you have to be loyal. This almost sounds like a marriage—but I see my coworkers more than I see my family at times. After working with a group of people for twenty years it was just like a marriage.

Effective team players know they have to communicate information to the entire team on what has to be done. Each supervisor involved with an assignment needs to have a clear understanding of what they need to get done. I have seen teams take responsibility for getting an assignment done without the supervisor having any knowledge of it. That means the middle manager did not communicate with the supervisor.

First of all, it is rude not to tell the direct supervisor. Second, the supervisor is responsible for their employees—how can they hold their employees accountable if they don't know what they should be doing? I see this too many times in production. The communication is bad and it causes more problems and confusion than I care to deal with.

I once had a superintendent who refused to let me know the details of an assignment and wouldn't give me any instruction on what we needed to do. This superintendent decided he would go directly to my lead person. My lead person missed some things and our manager (the superintendent's boss) wanted to know why. I explained to him that I had not received any instructions and that the superintendent went directly to the lead person. I didn't know they had missed anything because I didn't get the information. If I had known what was needed, I could have made sure it was done.

I worked in another location where all the supervisors were new and so was the superintendent. This guy would bring his supervisors in two hours early to work but tell them absolutely nothing when they got there. Time is one thing that you can never get back, and he was wasting his employee's time—time they could have spent with their families. I asked the superintendent what his game plan was. I was floored by his answer. He looked at me and said, "They can figure it out just like I did." Boy, did I have a sour look on my face. I couldn't believe someone who worked for our company had that kind of mentality. I had been around him and he had received information that his supervisors needed to get orders out. We were on the night shift and cuts were made in order for them to get all the orders out.

As soon as we started to run product, his supervisors were running product they didn't need. I asked the superintendent how he thought his employees would know not to run that product if he didn't tell them. He just shrugged. All I could ask myself was *who trained him?* I didn't learn my job this way. My manager was one of the best listeners and communicators I had ever met in my life. If he couldn't explain it to you, he would draw it for you. My manager would give the group an assignment, ask what we needed to complete the assignment, and ask us if we saw any problems or had any concerns. We were told to notify him immediately if anything changed after we made our final plan. He gave his team EVERYTHING they needed to reach their goal.

I was concerned about how this superintendent was treating his supervisors. This man worked for our company and all he did was stress out his supervisors. It was like he was running his own company within our company. Our company cared about all of their employees, in every position. This superintendent did not care. Someone had treated him like this. He didn't know what I knew. He didn't know this was wrong. I knew none of his supervisors would last. None of them had the proper training or treatment. This hurt my heart.

Later, the supervisor and I ate lunch with his coworkers. I had never seen a group of people who looked so sad. They were sad because every day they came to work they felt like failures, never winning. The morale was so low. It wasn't because of our company; it was because of their untrained superintendent. He didn't understand that what he was doing was giving our company a bad name.

Before I left this location, I gave some of the supervisors my number and encouraged them to call me whenever they had a question or needed encouragement. I knew it would be hard for them to continue working for our company. They were not getting the training and support they needed, so they didn't feel they were a part of our team.

Teammates train together, strategize together, play together, lose together, and win together. The coach leads the team. How can you win the game with a coach who does not follow the rules of the game? How can you win with a coach that does not want to play with the team? You can't win because you don't have what it takes to win.

How could these supervisors train their employees when they did not have the proper training? These supervisors were tired and frustrated. Our company did not operate this way; we believed in giving all of our employees the tools that they needed to get the job done. Our company wanted their employees to be successful and this individual was doing things his way and in the process he was affecting lives. He was young and inexperienced. He needed training. He was superior to me but I still felt like I had to tell him that he was not following the company vision statement. But this man was stubborn. He did not have respect for his coworkers, nor was he loyal to our company. He did things the way he wanted to, with little care for or patience with his new supervisors.

I stopped talking to him and went into my designated area and worked with the supervisor there. I spoke with each and every one of his hourly employees on the first day I was there. I found out so much about them, and their supervisor did, too. These employees had skills that were very useful. One of them was from a city near my home and his supervisor never knew. I was twelve hours away from my home and I was standing in front of an employee who was from an area less than an hour from my home. His supervisor never knew because he had never had a conversation with this employee.

Chapter 8 Questions to Consider

1. Do you feel like you are a part of the team?

2. Do you feel like you can communicate with your coworkers to accomplish goals?

3. Do you have a good working relationship with your coworkers?

4. Does your direct boss communicate information well to you and your coworkers?

5. Does your direct boss make you feel like you are a part of a winning team?

6. Are you doing everything you can to contribute to the success of the team?

Chapter 8 Points to Ponder

1. Be patient, communicate, compromise, respect, and be loyal to your co-workers.

2. Supervisors are responsible for employees.

3. Supervisors need all available information to get their job done.

4. Supervisors need proper training.

5. Motivate and encourage your teammates. Sometimes we all have bad days. Encouragement from your coworkers always helps.

Chapter 9: Superintendents Set the Tone

After seeing that untrained superintendent destroy any hope of those supervisors staying with our company, I was disturbed. I couldn't believe that he did not understand his position. I'm sure people in his position have a set of job duties they should be following, because they have a very important job.

Superintendents are the face of their entire team. They need to be knowledgeable and understanding. A bad superintendent can destroy a team and cause the company to lose money. Supervisors have to be able to communicate with their superintendent. I have had superintendents who intentionally kept information from me. What they did not realize was that I was responsible for my employees. When employees have an assignment, supervisors communicate it to them, give them what they need, and assist by supervising them. If a supervisor has given their employees a plan, how can they supervise the plan if the plan is changed without their knowledge? This causes confusion and countless mistakes.

Supervisors should be notified of any information that affects their team. I had an incident where I wasn't notified of a change and our manager asked me "How did we end up missing a truck?" I hadn't received the information that the truck was an early truck. My lead person forgot the superintendent had told him the truck was early. And most important, the superintendent got busy with a piece of broken equipment and didn't follow up with the lead person.

All I could say was that my employees had received information directly from the superintendent and I had no knowledge of the change. My response sounded stupid and irresponsible but it was true. If you are a production superintendent, understand that your supervisor needs you. Supervisors have to handle employee relations in the department. Who handles what the supervisor needs? The superintendent. And if superintendents need help, they should go to their manager.

Superintendents should organize the setup and make decisions based on the entire department, not just one particular area. When you organize the game plan on how you are going to run, involve all the supervisors. That way if someone has a problem, it can be communicated throughout the entire team.

During the course of the day, the superintendent should be somewhere in the department or notify their supervisors if they are not. If you know anything about production, you know things can change really fast. Supervisors need to make swift changes when there is downtime. If the change will affect the game plan, the supervisor needs to notify the superintendent immediately in case the superintendent has to adjust something.

Finally, superintendents should not show favoritism with employees. Every superintendent has supervisors. When a superintendent shows favoritism they lose respect, trust, and loyalty from their supervisors. If you are a superintendent, hold your supervisors to company standards and coach them as necessary and you will have an effective supervisor.

Chapter 9 Questions to Consider

1. Are you setting a good example as a superintendent or manager?

2. Do you understand you are responsible for your supervisors or superintendents?

3. Do you communicate information to your entire team?

4. Are you giving your supervisors or superintendents everything they need?

5. Are you fair?

6. Do you follow your company's vision statement, mission statement, and ground rules?

Chapter 9 Points to Ponder

1. Be a good leader and set a good example.

2. Superintendents are the face of the department. Superintendents need to be knowledgeable and understanding.

3. Give your supervisors all the necessary information and tools to complete a task.

4. Communicate with your entire team on matters that will affect them and their employees.

5. Let your supervisors know how to locate you when they need you.

6. Make everyone feel a part of the team. Don't show favoritism.

7. Expect your supervisors to do their jobs after you train them. Hold them accountable.

8. Give your supervisors a clear understanding about things that relate to them and their department.

9. Care about what you do. Don't act as if you are there just for your salary.

10. Direct, motivate, encourage, and inspire your supervisors.

Chapter 10: Points of Operation (Find The Root)

After working in production for more than twenty years and training hundreds of employees, I had learned a lot about the production process—but I was missing something. When I figured out what I was missing, the revelation was so wonderful. I learned how to look at my process through a system that I called *points of operation*. Points of operation immediately helps you find the root of your problem.

Employees in stationary positions can show you the root of a problem. Employees that are involved in fixing problems can help you eliminate problems because they can assist you in training others.

If you are a supervisor, sometimes you are asked to fix problems that are totally out of your control. I was in this situation and was adding extra staffing to cover problems that needed to be fixed from the root. I know I am not a rocket scientist—and it doesn't take one to do my job—but sometimes it almost seems like it would. Let me give you a simple scenario. If my company says we need to process 125,440 chickens and it should take eight hours, but it takes ten hours, what would you think would happen if a supervisor wasn't there during the process? All we had to do was process the chicken, pack it and ship it. There are only two reasons why it would take ten hours instead of eight: either someone messed up or someone was inexperienced.

Managers might give excuses, but the fact is that even managers screw up sometimes. It is very easy to scream "Fix the problem"—but when your supervisor doesn't have anything to do with the root of the problem, they can't fix the problem. Your supervisor can put a Band-Aid on the problem and continue to run up cost. Supervisors who are not directly in charge of a problem can't fix it unless they involve someone higher in management, but this can cause conflicts. You can't expect the processing supervisor to fix the packing supervisor's problem unless the packing supervisor is the one who is causing the problem. The best way to get to the root of a problem is to first identify the problem. Next, ask why the person is having the problem. Then, involve the most knowledgeable people to help fix the problem and train others so that they can be knowledgeable as well.

As a supervisor, you have to learn how to manage your department so that you do not affect other departments or your departmental cost. Knowing the points of operation in your department is absolutely critical for your success. I once ran a tray packing department. I discovered that I only had four points of operation in my department: the employee in the front catching the product, the employee stacking the product, the employee pushing the product to the scale, and the scale employee where I got my credit from.

I almost laughed out loud to myself when I realized how easy it was to understand my process by using my points of operation system. I had been looking at this situation in the wrong way for years. I had been distracted by the problems. I didn't realize all I had to do was find the root and fix one problem at a time. Any point of my operation would tell me why my product was not going into production. This didn't involve using extra staffing—it only involved eliminating problems at the root. All I had to do was have my employees that were in those spots trained. This is why training is so important. Your employees should know everything about their position, including all potential problems.

When I started to operate with my points of operation system, it gave me more time to deal with actual problems and fix them immediately. I found roots to problems I hadn't seen as major problems before. Most of my problems were caused by miscommunication. I was even able to get to the root of the mechanical problems. I started to look at points of operation in other areas and I even shared this revelation with other supervisors. I don't know if they were as passionate about this as I was, but I was ecstatic! I had had lots of good days with my team, but I after I discovered this system I began to have much better days. This system forced me to change my way of thinking. I was a lot more confident because I could now find the problems in my area and involve the most knowledgeable people to assist me in getting them fixed.

Don't ever feel stupid asking for help. I was in another department and the supervisor had thirty minutes of downtime, but once the right person was called it took less than five minutes to fix the problem because he knew what to do. The person who was called fixed the problem and then trained everyone around at the time how to fix that particular problem if it ever happened again.

Chapter 10 Questions to Consider

1. Do you know the points of operations in your department?

2. Is your department competitive in the area of cost?

3. Do you fix problems one at a time?

4. Do you fix problems or eliminate them?

5. Do you involve the most knowledgeable people to help eliminate problems?

Chapter 10 Points to Ponder

1. Know your process and each direct point that can stop your process.

2. Develop a system and don't make things complicated. Complications cause time and money.

3. Fix one problem at a time, making sure things are running right.

4. Get to the root of a problem and only involve the root when fixing the problem.

5. Hold employees accountable.

6. Teach floor men and rework employees all departmental jobs. These employees will keep your direct points of operations running smoothly.

Chapter 11: Conflicts and Problem Solving

There are three reasons why employees don't do their jobs. The first one is they don't have what they need. As a supervisor, when you check your points of operation always make sure your employees have what they need. The second reason is that the employee doesn't know how to do the job, and this is why you should give the very best job training. Utilize the experienced employees in your department to assist you in training new employees. Yes, a supervisor needs to monitor new employees' progress, but a person who does the job every single day will be able to train a new employee and get them comfortable with their position. I have employees that have done the same job for the past fifteen years. Those employees can tell me every aspect of that job because they have so much experience.

Now if you are not as fortunate as I have been and you don't have experienced employees, it is up to you to recognize talent, skill, and ability to position your employees where they can best help the company. You have to train them right the first time—because if you train them wrong, you will have to work extra hard to get them to do the job right. Training is so important. It sets the standard for the goals you are trying to achieve.

Simplify things as much as possible while training. Your production workers do not need you talking over their heads. Make their job as easy as possible. Give examples anyone can relate to. Some people may think that this sounds stupid but we use something we call a *cut sheet*—some people call it a *run sheet*. The cut sheet told management what orders we had and what time trucks had to leave. I would always use my experience as a fast food worker as a way to explain this sheet to new supervisors I was training. Back then, I used the comparison of customers waiting in line to represent the trucks waiting, and hamburgers and fries to represent product that had to go on those trucks. Now anyone knows that if you paid for a hamburger and fries, you are not going to leave with something missing out of your bag. And most people know that fast food orders go out first come first serve. The cut sheet has orders from earliest delivery to latest delivery. I was successful with training people in this manner.

Do what works for your team. If you are responsible for a team you should have a clear understanding of what you and your team are responsible for. That means that you should be able to train your employees if you need to. Everyone is an asset to the company unless they don't want to do the job. If the pay, benefits, position, policies, or supervisor can't motivate an employee, then maybe your company is not the company for them.

I understand that we as supervisors need to try to motivate our employees, but if they just don't want to work or follow the job requirements you need to enforce the company policy. My company employed about 1400 employees at our location. I would never risks losing money for those 1400 people by letting any employee not follow job requirements. What I am saying is that whatever company you work for, you need to do your job correctly because too many lives are affected if you don't. I don't care if you are in a higher level position or a lower level position. Companies should never tolerate mediocre performance. The bottom line is at stake, and that affects everyone.

I once had a 70-year-old employee who worked one job for more than 30 years and retired with no benefits. This employee had been with our company for 20 years and was a model employee. She came to work every day and she did a wonderful job. I couldn't let someone come in and do a bad job and risk her retirement, or mine. I was totally committed to what I did and my team needed to be also.

Sometimes things go wrong in your department that you can't control. These things may cause conflicts. When tackling a conflict that is out of control you have to follow certain steps in order to eliminate confusion. If this problem involves a supervisor, you need to go to that individual first. I know some coworkers are very difficult to deal with and no matter what you say it is never their fault. When you don't reach desired results with an individual you are having a conflict with, you need to follow your company's chain of command immediately. My company chain was supervisor, superintendent (also known as the middle manager), packing manager, plant manager, and division manager.

I had plenty of training from my division manager at the beginning of my management career, which was unusual. It was life changing for me, because most supervisors in my company were trained by a superintendent. But I was trained to look at things from a manager's point of view. The difference is that I had to deal with every day employee relations and I was hands on with the production side.

My manager and division manager gave me the start I needed to become successful. I was very young and inexperienced at the time and I never really thought about how involved they were in my life until years later. I loved them for what they did for me. They stepped in and they understood me. They gave me the support that I needed to do my job.

Middle managers can sometimes be the root of a supervisor's problem. When a middle manager does not properly train their supervisor they cause problems for employees and other supervisors. Middle managers don't have half of the employees to supervise that a production supervisor has. If you are a middle manager you are probably thinking you are responsible for two or three hundred people. No, you are responsible for your supervisors. They need you to communicate with them, explain things to them, make sure that they are trained, and be there when they need you. They need you to direct, motivate, encourage, inspire, and care. One of the most important positions in a production area is the direct floor middle manager or superintendent. This person sets the tone for the department.

Middle managers have to be well trained on company polices and it is critical that they have good communication skills. Middle managers can easily motivate a team, but they can also tear a team down. There is nothing worse than coming to work and knowing your boss is just there to get a check and thinks more about their position than their supervisors. This is what happens in most cases when a company brings a person in who has not invested anything into the company.

If you are a middle manager who has a bad attitude, you can't expect your supervisors to have good attitudes. You are training them. If you show favoritism, you have chosen your team and if everyone is not a part of it, it will show in production. And if you have not trained your supervisors to monitor, don't expect to get the best job out of your team because you won't.

Managers and middle managers can hold their supervisors accountable only after they have been trained properly and have experience. Supervisors need a clear understanding. Managers can't give them half the information they need and expect the job to be done right.

I believe that if supervisors are educated properly and given all the resources they need, their journey will be a lot easier and more successful than mine. If you are a supervisor, continue to learn, grow, compete, and strive to be number one.

Chapter 11 Questions to Consider

1. Do you know the three reasons why employees fail to do their job?

2. Do you make your employees' jobs as simple as possible?

3. Do you set standards for the goals you are trying to achieve from your employees?

4. Are you able to train employees if you need to?

5. Do you tolerate mediocre performance?

6. Do you expect your employees to do the job that is required of them?

7. Do you hold your employees accountable after they have been trained?

8. Do you know all of your company's policies and work rules, or know where to find them?

9. Do you motivate your employees by using your company's benefits?

10. Do you know your company's chain of command?

Chapter 11 Points to Ponder

1. Learn the company ground rules, fully understand them, and follow them.

2. Give every employee everything they need to do their jobs. Train them, give them the right tools, and support them when they have problems.

3. Simplify things—don't make a little problem a big problem by overthinking it.

4. Require all employees to do their assigned job correctly. Don't cut corners. Never tolerate mediocre job performance.

5. Follow the chain of command. If you don't know who is responsible, ask questions—don't assume.

6. Fix problems; don't patch them up.

7. Don't be a part of the problem—be a part of fixing the problem.

8. Be quick to fix problems. If you wait, you may lose opportunity and money.

Chapter 12: Four Point Management System for Retaining Hourly Employees

Being in a salaried position can be a difficult task sometimes, but with hourly employees who are trained and motivated anyone can build a successful team. I am very proud of the fact that I started out as an hourly employee. I saw my location go from mediocre to high performance. I remember what it was like when none of us knew what to do; what it was like to put in long hours of labor mentally and physically. I contributed to the growth of my company by working hard and training others the things I knew.

I have a number of hourly employees who have been under my supervision for 15 years. I have been successful with these employees and they have assisted me in training other hourly employees. I have developed a four point management system that can clearly and easily explain to you how to manage and retain your hourly employees.

Hourly employees can rarely change the environment their supervisor puts them in. It is the supervisor's job to train and motivate them. Every day won't be a good day, but with planning and preparation you can make things easier for you and your hourly employees.

Four Point Management System by Shaunta Mcdowell

1. Points of Operation

    A. Identify and train on all areas and positions that directly impact your bottom line.

    B. Clearly identify your support system for your points of operation.

    C. Train on consistently providing superior performance.

2. Delegating Responsibility and Recognizing Skills

    A. Wisely assign jobs based on skills.

    B. Utilize and develop employee skills for maximum contribution toward your business goals and objectives.

    C. Evaluate performance and make adjustments as necessary.

3. Motivating and Congratulating

    A. Always plan with a strategy to win. Let every employee know their position is important. Show them their value.

    B. Listen and develop a trusting relationship with your employees.

C. Give recognition when employees perform well. Celebrate goals achieved.

4. Holding People Accountable

   A. First priority in properly enforcing accountability is proper training. Ensure that your hourly employees are properly trained.

   B. Measure performance and ensure that jobs are performed to standard requirements.

   C. Manage performance and let employees know where they stand and what they need to improve. Always use disciplinary actions as a training tool.

5. Bonus: Emergency Action Plan

   A. Utilize your talent.

   B. Focus on solutions to problems that you can fix.

   C. Utilize outside resources.

Chapter 13: The Experienced Supervisor

As a supervisor you need to have tough skin—but sometimes in order to bring an employee's silent walls down, you have to let your heart talk. One day I had to fill in for a supervisor. I noticed product that was not going into production so I went to that area to see why. I asked the employee standing there what was going on and she just shrugged her shoulders. I could tell that this employee was frustrated. When I asked her if she was okay, she said, "I hate my job."

She said those words with such animosity. She was hurt. I asked her why she hated her job but she wouldn't open up and say why. She said, "I'm not mad, I just don't like this place." As I stood with her, I could visibly see some problems she was having as she was doing her job. Even though she wasn't my employee, I knew she was a good employee but I saw some things that were making her job difficult.

The employee said she had been working for the company for six years. At that point, I begin to discuss with her the benefits that were offered to her by our company. I encouraged her and let her know she was doing a great job.

Before I told her these things she couldn't see her benefits. All she saw was the things that made her feel unappreciated.

Sometimes all an employee needs is a little of your time to communicate with you. Now the walls were down because I spoke to her from the heart. She wanted to be told that she was a good employee because of the time and energy she put into the job. She wanted to be able to do her job with ease. I understood where she was coming from, because I was looking at some things that could be fixed but that she didn't have the power to fix and didn't know how. After I addressed one of her smaller problems with my coworkers, I was able to fix it. My coworkers were not requiring their employees to do their job correctly, which directly affected this employee. The problem was not coming from the company; it was coming from someone else not doing their job properly.

Earlier, I mentioned that people in a company are all linked together whether we like it or not. This employee's coworkers were making her life miserable and she was blaming the entire company. The face that she put on her problem was the company. As an experienced supervisor, you will learn to supervise with your heart. The employees that were not doing their job correctly needed a warning, and if the mediocre behavior continued, they would need disciplinary action.

Early in my career I didn't utilize disciplinary action like I should have. Later, I learned to use disciplinary action as an opportunity to communicate to an employee how they could do better. My goal now is for every employee to leave my office having learned how to do their job more effectively, and to not be upset—after all, you can't win them all. I want to explain to them what they did wrong. I want them to know how they can get better and how this experience can benefit them later.

With everything in life that you do—sports, school, or job duties—you have requirements. I have never terminated an employee. When an employee does not meet the company requirements, they terminate themselves. If we do not require employees to do their jobs correctly it will affect others. This is why you have a great opportunity with a new employee. New employees are a fresh start and a new beginning. If you train them to meet the company requirements, most likely you will have a long term employee. Retention of employees is important. It saves time, money, and resources. As an experienced supervisor I am more patient than I used to be—but as I have said before, mediocre performance can never be tolerated. Your career depends on you and others around you following job requirements and doing the very BEST job they can do.

Chapter 13 Questions to Consider

1. Do you know how to have tough skin with a heart to listen?

2. Do you recognize when an employee is having problems and needs your assistance?

3. Do you tell your employees when they do a good job and have you showed them that you appreciate their hard work?

4. Do you notify your coworkers when their employees affect your employee's job duties?

5. Do you believe that all employees are linked together mangers, superintendents, supervisors and hourly employees?

6. Do your employees know their job requirements?

7. Do you require your employee's to do their job correctly?

8. Do you have any long term employee's and have you communicated with them lately?

9. Do you have any new employees and are you giving them the absolute best training?

10. Are you satisfied with the way that your department is running?

Chapter 13 Points to Ponder

1. Notice problems your employees are having.

2. Notice changes in your employees and communicate with them on any visible changes.

3. Let employees know their company benefits—sometimes they don't listen during orientation.

4. Fix problems promptly. If you can't fix the problem, let the employee know you are working on it. Use other resources such as your boss.

5. Tell your employees they do a good job. They need to hear it.

6. Require employees to do their assigned job correctly.

7. Utilize progressive disciplinary action as an educational tool. Educate: Tell the employee what they did wrong and then tell them how it should be done. Motivate: Inform the employee of the next step if there is a reoccurrence, but assure them they can grow from the mistake they made. Inspire: Give encouraging words to the employee such as "You can do this. I believe in you."

www.ingramcontent.com/pod-product-compliance
Lightning Source LLC
Chambersburg PA
CBHW071934240426
43668CB00038B/1796